WHAT COLOUR IS A
BANANA?

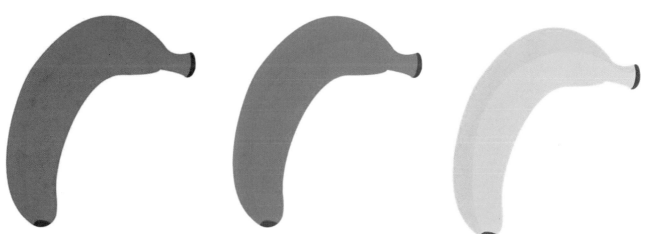

A BANANA IS YELLOW!

WHICH OF THESE LIVES ON A FARM?

A COW

LIVES ON A FARM!

WHAT DOES A **MOUSE** SAY?

A **MOUSE** SAYS...

SQUEAK!

WHAT COLOUR IS A PUMPKIN?

A PUMPKIN

IS

ORANGE!

WHICH OF THESE COMES OUT AT NIGHT?

THE MOON

COMES OUT AT NIGHT!

WHAT COLOUR IS A BEAR?

A BEAR IS BROWN!

WHICH ONE IS A FORK?

THIS IS A
FORK!

WHAT DOES A **DUCK** SAY?

QUACK!

A DUCK SAYS...

WHICH OF THESE LIVES IN THE SEA?

A FISH

LIVES IN THE SEA!

WHICH OF THESE IS A TREE?

THIS IS A
TREE!

WHAT DOES A **CAT** SAY?

MEOW!

A CAT SAYS...

WHAT COLOUR IS A TORTOISE?

A TORTOISE IS GREEN!

WHAT COLOUR IS A TOMATO?

A TOMATO IS RED!

WHICH OF THESE LIVES IN THE FOREST?

A
SQUIRREL
LIVES IN THE FOREST!

WHAT COLOUR IS A CARROT?

A CARROT IS

ORANGE!

WHAT DOES A SHEEP SAY?

A **SHEEP** SAYS...

BAH-BAH!

WHAT COLOUR IS A FIRE TRUCK?

A FIRE TRUCK IS

RED!

WHICH OF THESE CAN FLY?

A BIRD
CAN FLY!

WHAT COLOUR IS A BEE?

A

BEE

IS

BLACK

&

YELLOW!

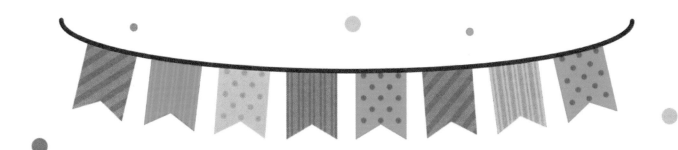

THE END!

BOOKS for little ONES

Find us on Amazon!

Discover all of the titles available in our store; including these below...

Test your knowledge further with another fun quiz book!

Full of questions about colours, shapes, shadows and sounds!

Images and vectors by freepix, Macrovector, RosaPuchalt, brgfx, lexamer, stephanie2212, lesyaskripak, Ajipebriana, cornecoba, omegapics, Rayzong, layerace, ddraw, Vectortwins, Vector4free, anggar3ind, iconicbestiary, freshgraphix, natalka_dmitrova, Anindyanfitri, Alliesinteractive, bakar015, johndory, VVstudio,

Made in the USA
Middletown, DE
09 December 2019